MR. MEN   LITTLE MISS

MR. MEN™ LITTLE MISS™ © THOIP (a SANRIO company)

Mr Happy and the Office Party © 2017 THOIP (a SANRIO company)
Printed and published under licence from Price Stern Sloan, Inc., Los Angeles.
Published in Great Britain by Egmont UK Limited
The Yellow Building, 1 Nicholas Road, London W11 4AN

ISBN 978 1 4052 8872 9
68156/1
Printed in Italy

MR. HAPPY
AND THE
OFFICE PARTY

Roger Hargreaves

Original concept and illustrations by
Roger Hargreaves

Written by
Sarah Daykin, Lizzie Daykin and Liz Bankes

EGMONT

Mr Happy was usually a very happy fellow.

But this was the morning after the office party, and Mr Happy didn't feel quite so happy.

In fact he felt like elephants were stamping on his brain and like he might be sick.

This is the story of how it happened . . .

It was another normal day in the office. Mr Grumble was grumbling about the printer, Little Miss Chatterbox was chattering at the water cooler and Little Miss Bossy had called a meeting about meetings about the new meeting process for meetings.

Mr Happy and Little Miss Magic had spent the first hour of the day emailing each other funny cat pictures.

The boss Mr Uppity, a self-made man who'd built his company from nothing but his father's millions, made an announcement.

'Tonight there will be an office party, with free drinks for everyone!' he declared.

'One plastic cupful per staff member,' he said, quickly backing into his solid gold office.

Little Miss Organised Fun appointed herself 'Head of Party Games' and enforced a strict fancy dress code. 'You have to join in or you'll spoil it for everyone,' she sang.

All the Little Misses rushed to the ladies' loo to fight over the one mirror, the one plug socket, and the one chance to attract the one vaguely attractive Mr Man in the office.

But it wasn't only the Little Misses making an effort – Mr Silly had donned his comedy tie, which was just as hilarious as it was the year before.

'It's so nice to get away from work!' said Mr Small Talk, as they stood around the office talking about work.

Mr Happy made a beeline for the one bowl of crisps, but got cornered by Little Miss Chatterbox. 'My youngest is potty training and has a tooth coming through,' she said. 'Do you want to see a video of him playing Frère Jacques on the xylophone?'

They all danced awkwardly in a circle and hoped the boss would leave soon.

Mr Fussy put in an appearance only to say he wouldn't be attending the party.

He was just there to put a note on the fridge saying:

'Would the individual who keeps using MY soya milk kindly deposit 87p on my desk. I buy this milk specifically because I am highly intolerant and gastro-intestinal distress is not a laughing matter.'

'I hope you catch the thief!' said Mr Happy laughing. 'Perhaps it's the same person who takes all the forks.'

Do you know where all the forks go?

Mr Grumpy also didn't want to be there. He had made it clear he was not a 'party person'.

And so he wasn't best pleased when he was selected as one of the contestants in Little Miss Organised Fun's Office Crystal Maze.

When Mr Happy finally escaped from the Aztec zone (stationery cupboard), he went to find Little Miss Magic. For some reason the office party always seemed a lot more fun when he was with her. But instead he got stuck talking to Mr Noisy.

Mr Noisy had a habit of talking very loudly, and had no sense of personal space.

'HAVEN'T SEEN YOU IN A WHILE!' shouted Mr Noisy. 'NOT AVOIDING ME ARE YOU?'

He also had halitosis.

Little Miss Magic seemed to have vanished, so Mr Happy went to talk to the new guy, who appeared to be drinking alone.

'Don't think we've met – I'm Mr Happy,' he said. 'What's your name?'

'Mr Nobody?' the man said. 'From Accounts? I've worked here for ten years!'

'Of course! I know who you are,' said Mr Happy, instantly forgetting the man's name.

The one bowl of crisps was running dangerously low, so Mr Happy went to find Mr Mean, who was in charge of petty cash.

'These are times of austerity,' said Mr Mean. 'We just don't have the funds for these sorts of things. We've all got to tighten our belts.'

Mr Mean then excused himself, saying he had to go and check on something.

Mr Funny, the self-proclaimed office comedian, silenced the party once again with an inappropriate joke.

And everyone tried to ignore the elephant in the room.

Mr Happy wondered if 5.30 was too early to leave. But then Little Miss Magic appeared, as if by sorcery.

'Sausage roll?' she said, holding out a platter of snacks.

'How did you get those?' said Mr Happy. 'You've got enough to feed the five thousand.'

'Magic!' she replied. 'Now let's go turn some water into wine.'

And off they went, narrowly escaping Mr Tickle's wandering hands.

Little Miss Magic introduced Mr Happy to her friend Magic Dave from Sales, who was a wizard at getting the party started.

The see-through man from Accounts appeared next to them.

'Who's your friend?' said Dave.

'Um . . . this is Mr . . . um . . . Mr . . .'

'Mr Nobody!' said Mr Nobody.

'Can I get anyone a drink?' said Dave.

Mr Happy nodded. What harm could one more drink do?

Mr Happy didn't remember anything after that.

But when he finally arrived at work the next day, Little Miss Chatterbox was more than happy to fill him in.

Mr Happy watched in horror as she showed him a video of him twerking on Mr Uppity's desk.

There was only one thing that could save him now. He headed straight for the biscuit tin . . .

It was empty.

'Looking for these?' said Little Miss Magic, snapping him back to reality. She was holding a packet of Hobnobs.

'Where did y-? How . . . ?' stuttered Mr Happy.

'Magic! Not really – I keep them in here,' she said opening a drawer full of biscuits, soya milk and forks.

For the first time that day, Mr Happy smiled.

He smiled again when Mr Mean was transferred to the Kuwait office and they were able to buy as many crisps as they liked.

But do you know what made him smile the most?

. . . when Little Miss Magic gave him access to her drawers.